UNLOCK
The Wealth of Talent

WORKFORCE INITIATIVES YOU CAN USE NOW TO MAXIMIZE YOUR COMPANY'S TALENT ADVANTAGE

HOW TO IMPROVE ORGANIZATIONAL EFFECTIVENESS BY IMPROVING PEOPLE OPERATIONS

By Margaret Graziano

CONTENTS

DEDICATION

I dedicate this book to my granddaughter Sophia Danielle for being my 'Why' and inspiration.

I would also like to dedicate this book to my first apprentice Dr. Stephanie Marberry PhD. Thank you for believing I had something to give. Your dedication gave Keen an opportunity to accelerate.

ACKNOWLEDGEMENTS

There are many people, programs and resources that influenced this book. Let me start by giving credit where credit is due.

Thank you for your mentoring guidance and vision.

Rose Graziano	DePaul University
William Graziano	Stephen Covey
Terry Petra	Ken Blanchard
Ginger Thaxton	Bruce Hodes
Joyce L. Gioia	Coaches Training Institute
Conrad Taylor	Rita Glass
Jeff Skrentny	Linkage
The Landmark Forum	John Mackey
Lifespring	Jack Canfield
Be Above Leadership	

Your wisdom trained me well, and now I get to give it away.

INTRODUCTION

If you have a notion that better people practices and a stronger culture will make a difference in your company's ability to achieve your goals, then the Wealth of Talent is the book for you.

The Wealth of Talent is designed for leaders who want to optimize their people, align their work culture and accelerate their company's business strategy. In this book, you will get a strong connection to the challenges plaguing corporate America, as well as defined, action-packed people and talent solutions that turn these challenges into competitive advantages.

TALENT SHORTAGE

Currently, the business workforce of America is experiencing a shortage of leadership talent, an issue that has been escalating due to aging Baby Boomers, for the last few decades. Other key triggers causing this talent shortage are the current global marketplace competing for talent, a weak disparate education system, the velocity and momentum of technology, and the ability for creative, innovative people to earn income from their kitchen table. If that isn't enough to disrupt the status quo; we are also dealing with the backlash of years of economic, political and institutional shakeups. The psychological impact of decades of uncertainty and perceived corporate and Wall Street deceit, as the pay versus cost of living disparity has triggered an all time low in U.S. employee engagement. With more and more companies needing to hire and the supply of qualified, engaged people at an all-time low, the result is a massive talent shortage of knowledgeable, committed workers who are available and interested in full-time gigs.

Fortune business editor Geoff Colvin said at a Staffing Industry Analysts Conference, "Upgrade your human capital. The only competitive advantage a company has is the people who work for and represent it. The best companies are seriously evaluating their talent pool and using this time to ask and tell the truth to themselves about who they have on their payroll and who they need to have. Now more than ever companies are evaluating and assessing their talent pool and continuing to measure their workforce performance quarterly. They are using this time to learn how to hire better people and to become proficient at proactively attracting and if need be stealing resources (people) from the competition." This is just as true today as it was 18 years ago.

A strategic initiative for many companies is to hire not only new talent but also the right talent. Given the shifting demographics facing us, companies committed to hiring top performers in their industry must create an environment that fosters growth, development, and challenge for its people. This behavioral and corporate transformation is referred to as adopting a talent mindset. This change in mindset empowers business leaders of progressive organizations to maximize the talent of their people and optimize its workforce. Running a company effectively now, and in the future is directly related to your ability to choose the right people for the proper roles, provide an environment for them to optimize their performance, and retain them for the right period of time.

A 2017 "Gallup Poll" on U.S. Workforce Engagement tells us that 70% of the U.S. workforce is disengaged—either by the work they do or by the place in which they do it. To drive home the adverse impact of a 15 year steady decline in employee engagement; data-driven production studies show that people who are unhappy at work are not nearly as productive as they could be, and are most often the same people who are unable, unaware, or unwilling to operate as proactive and innovative contributors. Disengaged employees are less likely to go the extra mile for customers or to improve workflows, organizational systems and processes that could streamline efforts and save your company time and money. These folks are also much less likely to have a positive impact on morale. In fact, they are often the key instigators of gossip and duplicity and are perpetrators of the blame/shame game in the workplace.

PEOPLE PRACTICES

Unwanted turnover can cause a disruption to a company's internal process and take an organization off track due to the impact that valuable people have on the organization. In an ideal world, the workforce in a company would be fully satisfied with their current role, invested in the company's mission, and see a clear path for their own success within the organization. This scenario is extremely rare, even among the best companies to work for. Investing in people practices can get your company focused on retaining those valuable employees and avoiding unwanted turnover.

When a company wants to impact their ability to hire and keep the best people, they must also consider the improvements needed on their management team and on the Recruitment process. If your management team does not possess effective employee engagement knowledge and does not fundamentally understand how to get the best out of people and leverage their strengths, you experience unwanted employee turnover and diminished returns on your people investments. Unwanted turnover also occurs when employees (specifically high performers) do not feel valued and appreciated for their unique contribution, or the focus is solely on the employee's current role, where there is little or no vision between their manager and themselves for their future within the organization. As they become more competent in the role, if new challenges are not available; they slowly lose their passion and engagement in the role and the firm, and over time become ineffective. Also, many bosses face the unprecedented challenge of having had little or no training in managing and engaging a multigenerational and disparate workforce.

On another front, the absence of many vital elements plague the modern-day recruiter and inhibit their ability to attract and draw in the right people. One is a weak or disjointed employment brand, while another is trying to recruit for a company that is out of touch with competitive salaries and employment packages for their marketplace. A major disconnect leading to concern for recruitment professionals today is when they are held accountable for employee retention, as in most cases they have no power or control once the offer is accepted. Furthermore, when the recruitment function does not influence new-hire onboarding and first-year performance management, failures in On-Boarding are often frustrating for both the recruiter and the management team.

The best companies educate their leaders on the competitive talent marketplace and adjust their offerings to enhance their employment brand. Additionally, these companies train their recruiters, including

---

Many bosses face the unprecedented challenge of having had little or no training in managing and engaging a multigenerational and disparate workforce.

the third-party and contract recruitment resources, to work inside their long-term talent strategy and align recruiting and hiring practices with the bigger vision, and values of the enterprise. Innovative companies are aware of the fact that employee retention indeed begins with appropriate recruitment and new-hire selection. What's new is that these companies are integrating (or embedding) specific retention-based talent management functions within the recruitment process, thus impacting the whole talent lifecycle.

Any company that values the power of their workforce fundamentally believes and operates congruently with those values and treats their people as their competitive advantage. These businesses are aware of the extenuating costs of replacing productive employees, and have systems in place to effectively integrate, develop and optimize the contribution of their people. Additionally, they take special consideration to elevate the employment experience throughout the enterprise. Progressive talent mindset companies do this by implementing customized onboarding programs, tailored employee development models, succession planning that considers both sides of the equation, employer and employee, and laser-focused performance management / performance coaching systems. In these leading organizations, the recruitment and employee selection process is built and managed with the end in mind—and that end is an optimized, engaged workforce. As the employment marketplace continues to heat up, companies choosing to compete in the marketplace through the quality of their workforce must learn to dance with an appeal to candidate motivations from day one—particularly to those who are high-impact (highly skilled, people facing, knowledge-base) workers such as salespeople, engineers, and managers.

When it comes to aligning people with the mission of the organization and continuing to nurture higher levels of engagement and contribution; it is an ultimate game changer when companies competing for top talent get into the hearts and heads of their people and learn to understand what makes them tick. When this is done right, managers get to know their team members at a deeper level and together with them, create a vision for a positive future from day one. These same managers drive higher levels of participation in their team members growth and development because they put systems and structures in place that keep the mission, the plan, the performance agreements and development programs at the forefront of day-to-day interactions and communication. When the Manager is focused on empowering their people to succeed and the focus is on removing constraints to performance, team members are naturally more trusting of their leader.

Effective people practices is the secret to aligning people to the organizational strategy and therefore raising employee engagement and elevating performance. But is just one step in getting your people to work for you with the same passion and performance that the company was founded on. Sometimes, you need to go back to the roots of the organization and the systems that are in place that make the day-to-day tick.

ARCHAIC SYSTEMS

In order to maintain alignment and impact your people practices, you must also be willing to look at the current structure of your organization. When was the last time you looked at the systems in your company? Are they making jobs easier or harder on your workforce? This is an essential step in understanding what is holding your people back and what can push them forward to excel at what they do.

Often systems stay in place because no one stops long enough to consider his or her purpose or relevance to the business. Small to mid-sized companies encounter many difficulties while competing for the best talent, primarily because building a strategic human resource presence and leadership training program has not been a top priority. The problem is a big one —and a strategic, systemic one at that. Today and going forward, implementing systems and operating practices that maximize your ability to attract and retain the best employees is and will be paramount to your company's success.

Strengthening your organization's ability to appeal to the right people is not only about selecting the right hires —that's just the beginning. When recruiters work hard to get the right people, they must understand that great people expect to work for great organizations and great managers.

If you hire an A or B player and surround them with C and D employment and talent management practices, you are asking for unwanted employee turnover. Additionally, the people these new-hires work for -the managers- must understand their role in fostering employee engagement and contribution. Managers play a major role in creating or destroying engagement, specifically whether they are a micromanager or a chaotic, unorganized, fly-by-the-seat-of-their-pants manager, there is an impact on their team members. New systems need to be put in place to empower the manager to set people up for success and to guide them towards effectiveness.

When companies leverage their people's strengths and fully engage their work teams, they capitalize on the brainpower of their workforce while innovating faster, competing smarter, and achieving their corporate objectives sooner. In turn, their employees see themselves as integral to the company's success, and they envision themselves growing within the organization as they look toward the future.

Your company's ability to stay competitive in the marketplace hinges on these key elements of your Talent Strategy and Management Fulcrum.

1. The leadership team's ability to maximize the returns on the company's people investments

2. Management and Human Resources ability to identify, utilize and leverage the strengths of team members people

3. Organizational success at keeping people actively engaged and productive.

All of these issues go hand-in-hand and resolved by adopting a talent mindset. You must be willing to look at all human systems through this lens when adopting new systems or re-working old ones. To not do so is a disservice to the people you have already invested in. Committing to this practice will not only allow you to improve the day to day systems that drive your people, but it will also give you insight into who you hire. The cost of a mis-hire can be equally detrimental to a company.

COST OF A MISHIRE

Hiring the wrong people because you are "in a rush" to put a butt in a seat leads to more unwanted employee turnover, and that unwanted turnover comes at a high cost. To add insult to injury, the cost of doing nothing about a lousy hire far outweighs the cost of being pro-active and creating high-impact hiring solutions.

In today's heated climate to hire knowledgeable workers, companies have to pay top dollar to hire the right people and, in turn, have the right to know what they are getting for their money. Yes, companies have the right to expect a return on investment with each hire. Not having enough knowledgeable workers leads to longer product development cycles, reduced sales and revenues generated, fragmented customer service or impeded customer experience, stifled innovation, and eventually lost market share.

When you think about it, especially with regard towards bottom-line profitability and stakeholder equity, establishing a protocol to hire consciously is common sense. Beyond the systemic costs of a mis-hire; such as wasted time and energy of everyone involved, the cost of recruitment

19

and training add up. Recruiting Brand equity, both internally and externally diminishes with every refill or mis-hire. Beyond those financial and perception costs, other costs include productivity losses of the manager, the new hire, and the surrounding teammates. The squandered time and the distraction from bigger commitments only intensifies any already looming employee morale issues. Add in the cost of equipment, benefits, and unemployment insurance rates, and you can see where it equates to three to six times the initial salary.

Unfortunately, even though the cost of a mis-hire demonstrates the effects of wrong hire, many managers and companies shy away from accepting responsibility or outright deny the evidence of making a poor hire and in turn, tolerate subpar performance. When poor performance is accepted as the norm, it only makes matters worse as the organization who retains mishires and poor performers is labeled by its employees as being tolerant of poor performance.

Whether it is the wrong hire for the wrong job or a good hire in the wrong position, if it is a mismatch it costs a lot of money, time and goodwill for everyone involved. There is no reason for a company that is successful and profitable in other areas to then lose at the game of hiring. It is crucial for companies that can hire correctly, to do so; otherwise, you are shortchanging the rest of the pieces that are working.

What is Conscious Hiring™?

Conscious Hiring™ is the methodology that allows for companies to put their mission, vision and values into action in real-time. When managers are fully committed to a conscious hiring process, individual behavior and general company culture is elevated to a new and improved standard of accountability and efficiency. When people are consciously hired for their gifts and abilities, it reduces uncertainty, improves morale, and generates an unparalleled level of momentum and innovation.

Implementing a Standardized Hiring Process

When hiring, great companies take the time to define what high performance looks like in each and every role. They also take the time to define and articulate a road map for success and demonstrate how each role produces outcomes that impact the company overall. These same great companies also invest the time to articulate the right behaviors, attitudes, beliefs, values and emotional intelligence needed in the role for success. Through the Conscious Hiring™ process each role is aligned with the overall company mission, vision, core values and strategic outcomes.

When leaders in the organization have clarity on what they need from each role, and employees are educated and agree to accept the responsibility for producing specific measurable results in the role. Both parties consciously enter into an engagement that has much stronger success rates than typical hiring processes offer.

When expectations and agreements are managed up front, and all parties are in alignment with the 'what', 'why' and 'how' of a role workforce engagement and productivity flourish. A Conscious Hiring™ process affords both the hiring manager and the potential team member an opportunity to use multiple points of reference before making a hire.

1. Conducting a Role Analysis

This is where Conscious Hiring™ begins. All parties directly impacted by the role need to understand the Comprehensive Position Requirements, which begins with why the role exists and further defines accountability, area of focus and specific selection criteria of the ideal person for the role.

2. Build Your Talent Pipeline

Creating a large enough candidate pipeline is the second most important element in Conscious Hiring™. This gives the hiring manager a choice of up to three qualified, interested and suitable candidates. A proactive, assertive approach must accompany the detailed Comprehensive Position Requirements for a conscious hire to happen.

3. Work History Evaluation

The interviewing process must consist of an in-depth structured work history evaluation as well as a patterned values-based behavioral interview. The values-based behavioral interview hones in on the desired values-driven behaviors identified during the role analysis process.

4. Assessing the Candidate

Once the interviews are complete, candidates undergo a compliant and validated assessment tool that flushes out their core competencies, skills, values, motivators and emotional intelligence. The hiring manager can then compare what they learned in the interview to the metrics gathered through the non-biased assessment results to discern a candidate's fit for the role.

5. Always Check References

It's always good practice to contact previous supervisors, co-workers, customers, and peers and inquire as to what it was like to work with your candidate. Whether you conduct a work history reference or a name, rank and serial reference, or you dig deep and ask behavioral based questions it's important to be thorough. Many people think references are hard to attain, however in my 20 years in recruiting I've found where there is a will to understand, there is a way to gain the information.

6. Bonding and Engagement

Create engagement throughout the process by spending time with the candidate to review in detail the company mission, vision and values and how the successful execution of the role drives the mission forward. Another element of a potential new hire grounding process is to clearly outline what it is like working for the company. Sharing the corporate cultural behavioral norms as well as the manager's approach to leading people really gives the potential new hire a sense of what it will be like to work for the organization. The candidate then has the information to make a healthy employment choice.

7. Test Drive Your Candidate

Ask the candidate to do something that demonstrates their interest, competency, drive, and ambition for the role. The assignment should be congruent with the tasks required in the role and give the candidate an opportunity to showcase their abilities and talents. This assignment allows the Hiring manager insight into what the candidates work product looks like and if the candidate is a good fit for the role.

In a Conscious Hiring™ process, a pre-established system keeps everyone consistent and honest and paves the way for a stronger, better hire. When both recruiters and hiring managers follow a process in a consistent manner it allows the company to gather pertinent data on each candidate in the running. Moreover, a stable and steady process enables each candidate fair and unbiased consideration.

Note: If you plan on implementing the use of an assessment tool, or standardized hiring process, it is important to know that once you use it on one candidate for a specified role, the EEOC1[1] and

1   The U.S. Equal Employment Opportunity Commission (EEOC) is responsible for enforcing federal laws that make it illegal to discriminate against a job applicant or an employee because of the person's race, color, religion, sex (including pregnancy), national origin, age (40 or older), disability or genetic information. It is also illegal to discriminate against a person because the person complained about discrimination, filed a charge of discrimination, or participated in an employment discrimination investigation or lawsuit. Most employers with at least 15 employees are covered by EEOC laws (20 employees in age discrimination cases). Most labor unions and employment agencies are also covered. The laws apply to all types of work situations, including hiring, firing, promotions, harassment, training, wages, and benefits.

OFCCP[2] requires that you use it on all candidates for the same role until a point in time that the hiring process and or assessment is no longer deemed a valid indicator of role success. The bottom line is: if one candidate is put through the process, all candidates need to be put through the same process or someone can claim favoritism or discrimination in the hiring process.

Let's take a deeper look into what a Conscious Hiring™ program is and how it can enable you to select the right people, for the right role, for the right reasons.

---

2   The purpose of the Office of Federal Contract Compliance Programs is to enforce, for the benefit of job seekers and wage earners, the contractual promise of affirmative action and equal employment opportunity required of those who do business with the Federal government.

Job Description vs. Role Analysis

A 21st Century Workforce requires clarity of expectations and clear success indicators. What is traditionally referred to as a job description is, in Conscious Hiring™ training, referred to as the CPR. The Comprehensive Position Requirements document focuses on the reason the role exists, what the employee needs to do, who they need to be and how performance is measured in the role.

When first establishing and building an internal hiring process, consider your corporate mission, vision and values as well as your philosophy, culture and business strategy.

➢ **Define** the purpose of the positions that exist.

➢ **Debate** with peers and come to a resolution on the specific measurements of success in the role. Clarify how those measurements are achieved.

➢ **Determine** the right values, behaviors and competencies the ideal employee needs to possess for this role.

➢ **Ensure** you can articulate what these look like in the workplace for effective performance, and translate them to descriptive Key Performance Indicators.

Next, list the tasks and core functions necessary to accomplish your desired outcomes, and how long those tasks should take in an ideal situation. Lastly, brain-storm with the key stakeholders surrounding that role about what behaviors, attributes, strengths, competencies and values, as well as intellectual, character and emotional quotients the ideal person needs to show up with. Remember to list attributes that are mandatory for success, yet not scope the job so high that Superman himself wouldn't qualify. Once you think you know what it takes to be successful in the role, benchmark your existing team of solid performers who hold that type of role.

Leverage Data on Your Top Performers

Understanding your current top performers is an excellent way to establish the core elements of what makes a person a success-ful employee in that type of role with your company. Additionally, benchmarking your existing staff allows you to see the common denominator winning traits of your team and to uncover what is missing—the presence of which would make a difference. When you know what you want and what you need in each role, and you can measure and compare or contrast candidates to those measurements, hiring becomes much easier and much more effective.

Invest In Your Talent Search

With an in-depth hiring process, you need many more candi-dates than you did when you were hiring based on gut feel-ing. Spend the time and money to diversify the search. Utilize as many resources as you can to populate the top of the funnel and give you plenty of choices. It is important to consider alterna-tive talent mining resources as well; you might look at complete-ly different industries housing similar types of roles. Opening the search to new industries increases the likelihood of gener-ating a multitude of candidates.

A Conscious Hiring™ process considers experience to the degree that the person can perform the job, but it does not ignore the core of who a person is for words that fit on a resume. In your advertisement, consider not listing exact experience required. It is a given that all roles need some level of experience walking in the door. But companies that employ Conscious Hiring™ report that behaviors, competencies and values, as well as philosophi-cal alignment, trump exact expe-rience when it comes to hiring the right fit. All of these and more make it imperative to implement a well-established and structured Conscious Hiring™ process.

Using & Validating Assessments

The use of assessments for Employee selection is one of the fastest-growing sectors in human resources. Assessment tools of various sorts are used to evaluate everything from candidate motivations, values and behaviors to communication style, personality traits, skills, mental agility, and organizational ability. Knowing your needs and what the market offers enables you to choose the right assessment. Before engaging with assessment tools, ask yourself some questions:

➤ What does the job require?

➤ What do you want to measure from your applicant pool?

➤ What types of tests are available?

Some assessments focus on only one dimension, like mental acuity, skills or knowledge base. Others consider motivations, communication style or personality traits. Still others focus on skills and competencies. Typically, when companies are hiring highly skilled knowledge workers for software development, sales or management roles they are looking for that person to have the ability to perform the role and the capacity to work well with people throughout the customer life cycle.

Maximize Your Leaders

Interview your internal clients (the actual managers) to determine what they want to achieve from their people and how an assessment would measure the person's ability to accomplish those objectives. For many managers, it's important to have assessments that enable them to better mentor and coach their newly hired employees. Or they need a formalized assessment that allows them to understand how to motivate, fully empower and engage their staff. Additionally, managers might see a need for a tool to elevate their ability to allocate resources more effectively and optimize their workforce.

Tailor Your Assessments

The most powerful use of your money and time is choosing one assessment that can be applied to the whole human capital picture, from hiring through to succession planning and retention. This, however, is no small challenge. If you choose a single assessment, it is important to see evidence that it passes the validation process. On a side note, read the fine print because some company materials state that their assessment tool is not to be used as a hiring tool. Other assessment tools fail the four-fifths rule (a mandate that states that if four-fifths of a protected class doesn't score well on an assessment it could be determined as discriminatory).

The Power of Benchmarking

An excellent form of validation is benchmarking. When an assessment is given to over 100 top performers from different companies in a similar role, the benchmark validation is the average sum of the results in each category. You can also customize your benchmark by assessing 9 to 11 top performers in a specific role within your company, the same number of employees with mediocre performance, and another group of the same size with poor performance. Have someone analyze this data and distinguish the common denominators of strengths and weaknesses in each group, as well as highlight areas for growth opportunities and red flags that signal threats to effectiveness.

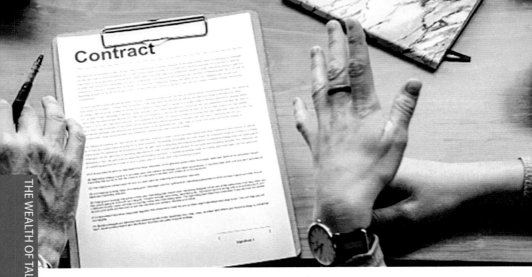

The Inner-viewing Process

A solid hiring process always consists of a standardized interview model, whether it is a top grading format (as mentioned before) or a work-history questionnaire. Before you start interviewing, ask these questions and ensure that any candidate who is participating in your selection process feels valued and respected:

> ➢ What is the objective of the interview?
>
> ➢ Are the selected interview questions appropriate for the role type and job category?
>
> ➢ Who do I need on the interviewing team?
>
> ➢ What do I need from them?

> ➢ Does everyone have the questions, and have they had a crash course in the interviewing model?

Interview vs. Inner-View

It is important to understand your candidate's track record, the types of companies they worked for, the roles they held, and how they went about producing results. But it's just as important to learn and understand how and why they made the decisions they did, what they liked and disliked about their companies and their jobs, and their history of progression or regression in their career. You are not only interviewing these candidates to determine if they can do the job and perform; you are also interviewing to determine if they are a good fit internally and externally, and how long they will stay engaged and productive.

In his management consulting work, the late Peter Drucker taught that often two-thirds of all hiring decisions are mistakes because many hiring decisions are made with inadequate information (**druckerinstitute.com**). When breakdowns in hiring occur, it is most likely because someone chooses to bypass the process and hire someone they think can deliver more than was originally advertised, and their instinct tells them to hire this person and bypass the process. Invariably, the decision maker is impressed by someone's credentials or charisma and ceases to lead the interview in an investigative manner. The interviewer switches to selling mode before uncovering all the key features, benefits, strengths and weaknesses this candidate comes with; in the end, neither the person nor the role delivers.

Regardless of a candidate's credentials or charisma, it is mindful business practice to include a structured, patterned interviewing model in your candidate credential validation process. This could be a behavioral-based interview or not.

Do's

➢ Ask open ended questions: The key is that the questions need to be open-ended and thought-provoking.

➢ Be specific about your ideal candidate: An Inner-View determines if this person has what it takes to perform the day-to-day functions of the role and deliver required results in the manner that suits your company culture, values, philosophy and mission. If character, intellect and emotional quotients are important for success in your organization, implement some level of validated behavioral interviewing system.

Don'ts

➢ Do not use generic material: Downloading questions off the Internet or take any sample questions out of resource material is inefficient: those are designed as examples and may not be a relevant line of questioning for the competencies, behaviors, modes of thinking, modes of interacting, modes of acting, or the motivations you require in your role.

THE WEALTH OF TALENT

A solid behavioral interviewing program gives you a menu of behaviors, competencies, values, methods of communication and modes of thinking to choose from. An equally solid decision-making rank-order matrix for the most important hiring criteria is a conscious minded way to measure and weigh the candidates as compared to the hiring criteria.

During the Inner-View process, make sure the interviewer is doing a minimal amount of talking. The purpose of the Inner-View is for the interviewer to understand the candidate, not for the interview to sell the opportunity; there is a time and a place for that and the Inner-View is not it. In the end, ensure that you measure your finalists against what you said you wanted in your comprehensive position requirements (developed during the role analysis process). If no one hits the mark, the right thing to do is generate more candidates until you have two or three that fit the bill.

Begin with the End in Mind

Understand	Identify	Get Results

Purpose of the Role | Key Performance Indicators | With Core Focus

Pre-employment Bonding

Pre-employment bonding always begins with a compelling employment brand. Effective assimilation starts with the first connection with the candidate before the interview process and continues through the first year of employment. From the moment a candidate speaks to someone from your organization, they are evaluating it and whether this is the right place for them. Is your EVP compelling and inspiring enough to capture the attention of the best candidates in the marketplace?

Part of being a top performer in business is discernment. Top performers vet the employer like the employer ought to be vetted; they typically reject a subpar opportunity upfront. If a solid performer accidentally finds themself amongst low-performing peers and managers, typically they are astute enough to leave before the opportunity adversely impacts them. Truly competent outward-facing knowledge workers who act in mission-critical roles don't need to apply for jobs with companies that don't care about their people or lack a talent mindset. They are savvy with their expectations for company culture, management philosophies and best practices. These key contributors expect their current and future employers to provide mutually beneficial work environments and competitive, employee-centric employment packages.[3]

The reality is that there are plentiful opportunities for sharp people with creative and outward facing skill sets who possess initiative, job ethic, personal accountability, common sense and emotional intelligence. If these are the people your business needs to hire, you need to master the art of attraction and be the people you want to find.

➤ Make certain that everyone, from your recruiting coordinator to your receptionist, knows that candidates are to be treated as customers.

➤ Ensure that whoever conducts the interview is engaged in their role and aligned with the company, as well as a good performer in their role and a good employee.

Prepare for Success

The interviewer needs to be given space to be emotionally and intellectually present for the interview

and during the interview. Often, the most damaging aspect of a company's employment brand is when a highly skilled candidate interviews with someone internally who treats them in a way that alters their experience of the perceived employment brand. Companies that adopt a customer service philosophy in recruiting always have more candidates applying than jobs available.

Streamline Your Follow Up

Once the offer is extended and accepted, it is very important to set up a system for communication from the point of acceptance to the start date. A great element of pre-employment bonding is to send a hiring kit. Include company literature, industry information, reading material, and testimonials from employees who have grown their careers within the organization. Additionally, have a new hire onboarding team set up and ready to go on the new hire's first day to ensure an effective transition into the new role.

---

3 An employment package refers to the complete employee offering, over and above salary, incentive pay and benefits. It includes offerings such as remote work opportunity, flex time, tuition reimbursement, mentorship programs, etc.

EMPLOYEE ENGAGEMENT

Onboarding

Now that you have implemented a Conscious Hiring™ process, it is imperative to establish a method for effectively integrating new-hires into the company. An introduction to the organization with a key executive and the management team is a crucial function, as it "reinforces the sale". Additionally, when done mindfully it creates a vision that connects the new hire, and their career path to the organizational goals and future state.

Workforce Strategy

There are eight vital elements instrumental to effective new hire integration that are best to accomplish during the first week or two of employment.

A meeting with a key executive is number one. When the executive generates their passion for the mission, vision and core values of the enterprise it is contagious and creates an opening for the new hire to catch the passion for the bigger picture. When the Chief Executive or Managing Partner shares their overall business and management philosophies, the company's position in the marketplace and their strategic objectives the new hire has the opportunity to explore with the Executive how their specific role plays a part in the overall system, the new hire immediately feels connected to the plan.

As the first few days progress, a fundamental element to the new-hire and the manager's relationship and working agreements is when they meet to come together and discuss the significance of the individual's contribution to the organization. In this discussion, the manager can get in to more detail as to the 'why' behind the hiring selection- why this specific individual was chosen, and why the role they perform matters to the organization's success.

Another vital element of the first few days is an office tour with introductions to people the new hire needs to know and works with directly. Having more than one person lead the orientation is a key element of a good onboarding program. When various levels of management and colleagues present themselves and their roles in the company, the normal culture shock that people experience when starting in a new company is eased; early bonding relationships are created.

Additionally, to enable a smooth transition and empower connectivity for the new hire, many progressive organizations assign a buddy, a sponsor, and or a mentor during the first 120 days of employment. Typically, a company committed to making new people feel part of the team arranges a lunch with the direct supervisor or the team surrounding the new hire. It is also a nice touch to have an onboarding gift either sent to your new team members home or waiting for them at the office. The gift could be as simple as a mug, a company shirt or any other company-logoed item; it also needs to include a written version of the mission, vision and values. There is no limit to how many times this needs to be shared with team members, frankly, in most organizations, this is done far too little, and people become numb to WHY the organization exists and how they play a part.

Once the formal onboarding program is in motion, the next step it is for hiring manager and supervisor to take it to the next level. It is very powerful when the lead of the Department or Business Unit creates a sense of ownership for the hire's role on the team. Clearly laying out how the department works with others in the company, and what its overall role in the human system is, gives the new team member an understanding of who they will be interacting with on a regular basis and who does what in the bigger scheme of things. When the Department leader reviews the objectives of their group and clearly articulates the specific key performance indicators (KPIs) for the new team members' role, it adds congruency and consistency in messaging around expectations and impact. Studies indicate that most people need to hear things 7 times before they commit it to memory; when organizational leaders keep this in mind and continually repeat a consistent message around performance and the big picture it brings clarity and freedom for both the new team member and the Manager. Hearing multiple times from various people why they specifically were chosen to join the team and the positive impact their role is required to make in the organization alleviates fears of the unknown and sets the new team member up for success.

Another key element in a solid onboarding program is when the Manager has an opportunity to expound on his or her management, communication and feedback style with the new team member, and gives the new hire the space and time to share how they prefer to be managed, developed and coached. When people know what to expect from each other, there are fewer surprises, and new hire integration is much smoother. Additionally, employee engagement flourishes in an environment where people are clear on what is expected and are set up to win from day one.

Drivers of Engagement

At the start of the 21st century, the majority of the United States experienced a major set back in the business world; so much that many companies needed to decimate their training budgets as one component of a survival strategy. Organizations who did survive the great recession operated lean and mean. Unfortunately, the problem with this approach is that over the last 15 years, poor management has become a leading cause of eroding employee engagement and unwanted employee turnover.

Evidence of this comes from studies by the likes of Gallop and McKinsey report that less than 18% of leaders actually have the skill to lead in today's world. Through leadership summits and surveys, Gallup has also determined that only 35% of managers are currently engaged in their role, and only 10% of the workforce have the skills required to lead. When managers are not given adequate training, mentoring or coaching on how to manage people, it impacts how they treat people and how people experience their work-life.

When interviewed, surveyed and asked most of today's

business managers say they feel ill equipped to do their job effectively. The lack of knowing what is important in leading people results in the managers' themselves being disengaged and disconnected to what really matters to their people. This results in people feeling like they are cogs in the wheel of a machine rather than valuable and contributing members of a team. As managers, it is important to understand and take responsibility for our impact on the people we manage.

This being said, relationship with the manager is only one of the top 10 top drivers of engagement that impact human beings experience of work. When it comes to employee retention and turning the tides of unwanted employee turnover, the results from HR Executive (**hreonline. com**), demonstrate the costs of such employee engagement erosion. In a survey from early 2015 it reports that 45% of all internal candidates' within an organization's pipeline are looking for opportunities elsewhere. [1] These results ought to cause a major concern for every kind of business leader, no matter the size, industry or geography.

The Workforce Institute 2015 Retention Report reveals that 76% of all employees leave their jobs for preventable reasons. With thousands of high-performing potentials all over the nation, this is somewhat surprising. In another employee poll conducted by Gallup, the results are just as compelling:

- ➤ **41%** of employees are not satisfied with their jobs
- ➤ **46%** say their workload has increased
- ➤ **33%** feel they're at a dead end at their current job
- ➤ **78%** believe they are coping with "burnout"
- ➤ **56%** are not glad they chose to work for their current employer
- ➤ **63%** think their top management displays neither integrity nor morality

The Cost of Disengagement

Gallup Poll metrics show that active disengagement of the workforce costs an estimated $450-550 billion per year in the United States. This equates to 4% of total revenue generated in the

US. With these numbers in mind, we can conclude that active disengagement is costing your organization 4% of revenues. To add depth to these statistics, the Millennial generation will compose 75% of the workforce by 2020, and one of the top drivers of this generation is to experience purpose and meaning in their work.

That being said the cost of not prioritizing the company's Mission and Purpose into every aspect of the human system causes palatable and preventable losses, both financially and energetically.

Future Workforce Trends

Forecasting from McKinsey Workforce Trends report tells us that we are facing a new era of workplace operations:

> ➢ Exponential scaling adoptions of tech-based practices, will lead to 33.5[2] [3]% of current activity hours becoming automated by 2030.

> ➢ Increase of automation in the workplace, 33.3% (one third) of the workforce will lead to significant occupational changes in the workforce population.

> ➢ An increase of retirees (65 years and older) will skyrocket from 14% in 2017 to 21% in 2030.

> ➢ The annual increase of GDP per capita will rise 1.3% between now and 2030.

In this new work environment, companies need to prioritize rethinking organizational design, and redesigning business processes. With the accelerated deployment of automation and AI, partnerships in talent development need to take place to build core digital and analytics capabilities. Adapting talent strategy and managing workforce transitions is paramount for businesses to remain competitive and efficient.

Reasons for Lack of Engagement

When employees come to work in the bodily form only (the physical person shows up, but the mind and heart are absent), we call this warm chair attrition (WCA). These people are at their desk, but most if not all days, they are not getting anything beyond ordinary done. They only produce at a reasonable level some of the time. Regardless of the impetus for their WCA, people who are aware they have warm chair attrition tell us they often bide their time until their "dream" job comes along. Those who operate with this mentality of "just doing enough" are often unaware of their impact on the organization.

Of course, this problem gets much more prominent in a larger organization, where often people and performance issues get lost, sometimes for years at a time.

Tracking warm chair attrition can be very valuable. Although it is essential to study, currently there is no data to analyze which percentage of WCA is caused because the person just was not a fit in the job or outgrew the role, or which is caused because a good employee was managed by a bad supervisor or vice versa.

When tenured folks feel cemented or want to feel cemented in a job or a company, they often start "corporate cocooning." Cocooning happens when the highly experienced worker stays in their silo and hoards information. These folks tell us it often occurs unconsciously and is because they like to be perfectionists; however, it might be deep-seeded insecurity about their value to the organization and are afraid to share with or train others for fear of being replaced. We often hear from workers who need information or need training and context that it is frustrating trying to work collaboratively with a cocooner.

If cocooning happens out of fear, people are justified in feeling this way. For years, seasoned workers have seen younger, higher skilled but less experienced people joining their companies and moving past them. Typically employees who corporate cocoon have tenure within a company, which means they have been working for some time. During the time when they came up through the ranks, people kept the same job for a long, long time. What could serve these cocooners is getting back to school, taking self-esteem classes, or engaging in a hobby that pays. No job is forever, and if you don't shift, you eventually need to leave.

The new age brings a new age problem for employers everywhere, and that is the "free agent mentality" (those who opt to work at home, part-time, or as independent contractors). These are often GenXers who have families and reasons they need flexibility. Their bosses know they are good workers, so they give them the freedom to balance their work and home life. What is often missed in these cases is that over time the employee and the hiring manager lose their connection and, if not built into the structure of the relationship, personal feedback and coaching fade away.

The demographic and psychographic challenges facing our companies cannot be avoided or ignored. In response to the issues of diminishing knowledge and shifting demographics in the workforce, many Fortune 1000 companies are putting systems in place to position themselves as employers of choice. In the SHRM national survey in 2012, results reported that the trend most likely to have a strategic impact on how human resources departments function is the growing need to develop retention strategies for mission-critical players, key contributors, and next-level leaders.

Preparing for an older workforce and the next wave of retirement was second on the list, planning for and managing labor shortages at all skill levels was third, and putting systems in place for employee growth and development such as succession planning and people readiness programs was fourth.

In the corporate world, retention is the power to keep employees actively engaged and committed to being an integral part of the organization. When a company does a great job of hiring the right people and retaining them, they maximize their ability to secure and maintain market share. Businesses that have cracked the code on recruitment and talent management hold on to customers longer and are in a position to proactively solve their customer's problems. Those companies are leaders in their industries by offering new and innovative solutions to their customers because of a steady stream of new knowledge and stable relationships. The correlation between employee retention and profitability is clear.

Strategic Applications for Talent Retention

Given the shifts that are taking place in the workforce and the needs that will need to be met in this new workplace environment, employers are becoming more innovative in recruiting and retaining employees - especially Millennials. A critical piece of the retention picture is when you as a manager understand your people. You need to know how they think, learn what is important to them, and get in tune with what makes them tick. The Society for Human Resources Management published a global engagement study, in which the following ten items came up as the most critical levers in driving employee engagement, as well as their absence being a major factor in causing disengagement:

➢ Confidence in organization's future (mission/vision)

➢ Promising future for oneself

➢ Company supports work/life balance

➢ Safety is a priority

➢ Excited about one's work

➢ Confidence in company's senior leaders

➢ Satisfied with recognition

➢ CSR efforts increase overall satisfaction

➢ Satisfied with on-the-job training

➢ Manager treats employee with respect and dignity

When looking at employee engagement, it is essential to understand and acknowledge that people are not all wired the same way. What is important to a seasoned veteran at 55 years of age is very different from what a 28-year-old business associate finds important. People are the sum of the life they have lived. Including the values they hold, the people they surround themselves with, the issues they dealt with while growing up, the era that they grew up in, and the behavioral and personality archetypes they adopted along the way. A strong manager sees this and manages different personality and work styles, while allocating the workload accordingly.

21st Century Workforce

Business unit leaders and managers are better equipped to do their job when they understand their people and what turns them on and off. Knowing this is only half the battle; doing something about it is what's important. The workforce is the company's internal audience, and that audience is diverse. Appealing to this diverse audience requires the ability to mirror their needs and wants, and blend those with your company's role and career offerings.

An effective way to demonstrate a talent mindset is in the hiring process. Define the purpose and passion of every position. The right person will be attracted to that purpose and passion. To engage your audience, you must sell them to come onboard, and continue to influence them to stay. In retention strategies, you learn to speak to each employee through their demographic and psychographic views. Here you learn their motivations and values and gain insight into their beliefs and why they act the way they do. Each person has different incentives and key motivating factors that speak to them.

Let's take a deeper look at the four generations influencing and populating the workforce today.

Please understand the Author is clear that these are sweeping generalizations and the purpose of this piece is not to stereotype people, it is simply here to give context to how the world of work is changing and what we can do about it.

Four Generations, One Workforce

Today, the workforce mostly consists of and is influenced by habits from World War II folks, born before 1946; the Baby Boomers, born from 1946 to 1964; Generation X, born from approximately 1965 to 1981; and the Millennials, born in the 80s and 90s. We know Gen Z is on the horizon; they however are still on the fringes of the workforce and for this purpose are not included in this synopsis. For each of these generations, we provide a look into what life was like for this generation when they were growing up and forming their perspectives about the world and the world of work. We also delve into what influenced each generation's behaviors and motivations:

WWII Generation

For WWIIers, times were hard, people were in survival mode, and a traditional lifestyle was sufficient. These folks grew up in the age of the assembly line,

the birth of labor unions, and in times where religious worship and regimen were the norms. Independence, entrepreneurism and freethinking were very far from the standard, and back then you took what was handed to you. The only way around it was compliance, service, and perseverance. Those who followed got to lead. Hard work, processes and a systematic plan were solutions to many of the world's problems. This generation shows care for people by providing food, shelter, stability, and structure. Words and conversations are not the most significant form of communication in the family realm, and in big business, religious organizations and community groups, it was the system itself that gave the sense of stability, not the relationships inside of the systems.

The WWII traditionalists have many valued qualities; one of the most potent is their stability. They know what they want and are satisfied keeping things in the norm. They are detail-oriented and believe that accuracy matters in a well-done and complete job. Thoroughness is an excellent asset. They are patient and hardworking, and you can count on them for jobs that require attention to "doing things right." Tasks that follow a methodical process over and over again (as is often needed in on-the-job training programs) typically are a good fit for this group.

Along with what this generation brings to the table, sometimes their behaviors don't work, especially with today's 21st-century workforce. Often this can be viewed as a liability. All in all, most people of this generation resist change; they do not feel comfortable bucking the system, and because they might be uncomfortable with conflict, they don't speak up even when it's needed. If you have these people on board as employees or are leasing their intelligence and experience as a consultant, mentor or coach, the messages you can use to motivate this group are:

"We respect your experience and wisdom."

"It's valuable for us to hear what has and hasn't worked in the past."

"Your perseverance is valued and will be rewarded."

The Baby Boomers

When these people were growing up, the U.S. had entered a new era—an era of freedom and growth. The Big War was over, and it was time for a change. The family unit was strong while this group was school-aged, but as they entered into adulthood a new kind of war had begun. The country came together with messages of peace, love, and experimentation. Hard work paid off, and many kids who grew up with nothing came into prosperity because of their work ethic, determination, and dedication. Most of this generation is very driven for success and willing to go the extra mile because while they were growing up, they were told: "we cannot afford it."

In their adult lives, they look to provide what they and their kids want, while they seek to accomplish and persevere. Most of this generation is good at relationship building. They measure themselves on the amount and types of relationships they nurture, work hard to please, are good team players, and need to know they are valued and worthy. One of the highly appreciated qualities of this group is their commitment to service and community building. This way of thinking may

be due to the "peace, love and rock and roll" that brought them together and united them against war, or because of the need for affirmation and acknowledgment from their WWII limited-communication parents. Now this most populous generation, the one with the most people in the workforce, are entering a point in their lives where they want to reduce the amount of time and energy they dedicate to their business life.

Along with all strengths come weaknesses, and this generation has both. They are often uncomfortable with conflict or going against the peer group. At times they may put the process ahead of the results. They do not like criticism and are known to take it personally. Boomers are often accused of being very judgmental toward people or alternative thinking. Probably the most common theme of weakness for this group is their self-centeredness (my family, my house, my car, my vacation, my life). This group is not naturally budget-minded (hence our country's financial position today). Many of these adults were raised by WWIIers and are not conscious of their intrinsic value. They often feel validated in earning and spending. If you have these people in your employ and want to keep them engaged, feeling valued and appreciated, messages that motivate this group could be:

"You're important to our success."

"You're valued here."

"Your contribution is unique and important."

"We need you."

"I approve of you."

"You're worthy."

Generation X

Growing up during the age of divorce, the GenXer may have been a latchkey kid, and often entertained, ate and did their homework by themselves while their parents worked. They watched their parents become workaholics, and assessed these priorities were unsuitable; they vowed that things would be different when they became parents. They have experienced the WWII bureaucracy blow up, been burned by government failings and lack of insurance, and were around during the birth of the Internet. They have friends who got rich with Apple, Google and Facebook and many of them feel they are left to lead business and government and fix what their predecessors have messed up.

The smallest population in the workforce, this group is the up and coming pool of managers and the prime age group for today's high potential recruits. They are typically highly skilled in their area of expertise. This generation may be the most cynical and resigned generation we have today. The problem is that they feel the leadership model currently in place is insufficient to meet the demands of the problems they have to solve. Generation X has many valued qualities: they are incredibly adaptable, very techno-literate, fiercely independent, and not intimidated by authority. They're often praised for their high level of creativity in the workplace.

Now for some of the negatives. GenXers are often seen as being impatient with processes, policy, and people. Employees and customers at times complain that they have poor people skills and act like they don't care; they often believe they are wiser than their years of experience, so at times make bad decisions. Their attitudes toward life and business can be cynical. If you have these people in your employ, high potential or management training programs messages that motivate and stimulate this group might be:

> *"OK, do it your way."*
>
> *"We've got the newest technology."*
>
> *"There aren't a lot of rules here."*
>
> *"We're very informal here."*

The Millennials

The second most-populated group and the most substantial influx of U.S. workers are the Millennials, whose average age is 20 to 35 in 2016. Raised in the high-speed Internet age and self-help era, they've had new information, both logical and psychological, to process since birth. They were school-aged when 9/11 happened and watched the Twin Towers collapse many times on television. In fact; terrorism, earthquakes, and tsunamis were all brought to them via the big screen. They saw the first black man in the U.S. become president, who got the job because he declared it and used the Internet to cause it. They had a digital device in their hands by the time they turned ten years old.

This group is highly techno-savvy and can multitask better than an octopus on steroids. They value collective action and team spirit, are heroic, and possess a healthy degree of tenacity. The Millennials want and need new challenges at light-year speed. The Millennials also believe they know more than any other generation including the errors of our world's ways. They presume their generation can fix whatever is broken through the invention of bigger and better solutions. They want to know about the problem and require the freedom to solve it with minimal systems, processes or procedures.

That said, here is where they struggle: they need supervision and structure, which is guaranteed to challenge their managers and co-workers, especially because they reject the old format of management, which tells them "Do what I say because I said so." They are fine with producing the results; however, they are certain their way is better, cheaper, faster and more creative. The good thing is that most of them acknowledge this and want the help. They tend to be inexperienced with people issues and are uncertain—if not unaware— of how to deal with conflict and authentic face-to-face communication. Often accused of having an extremely short attention span, they lack patience for mundane, menial, low-impact tasks. Hiring this group of fast-trackers is your future, and you can motivate them by saying:

"You'll be working with bright, creative people."

"We can put you on the fast track."

"Your computer is equipped with the latest and greatest graphics."

"You and your co-workers can help turn this company around."

"You can be a hero here."

Effectively Understanding Perspectives and Their Impact on Business

WWII types respect the Boomer work ethic, but that they often seem wasteful and self-centered. They often feel the generation of GenXers is not as hardworking as they were, and don't understand the value of team play; however, they acknowledge

that this group of workers has some pretty good ideas. When it comes to Millennials, the WWIIers admit these kids are technological wizards but wish they could concentrate better.

Baby Boomers share with us that they tend to view WWII traditionalists as narrow-minded and unwilling to adapt, but they recognize that WWIIers have wisdom to share and the know-how to get work done. They tend to believe that GenX can't balance it all, are needy and costly to train, and are preoccupied with continually wondering if they can do better. As for Millennials, while they see them as the future, they also wonder if the whole generation may have ADD.

GenXers view the WWII generation as a bunch of has-beens who should retire and, in doing so, roll out a companywide succession plan with fresh new faces and a new breed of leadership philosophies, skills, and abilities. They often share amongst their peers that their bosses are self-centered, recognition-seeking workaholics who don't care about or understand their people and often miss the big picture. Frequently, GenXers say the same thing about the

Millennials, which may be more of a reflection on Generation X than the generations they label. They observe that, while younger workers blow them away when it comes to multitasking and technical creativity, it is hard to talk to them and they have a know-it-all attitude.

Millennials tell us they respect the WWIIers and need their wisdom and understanding, but they want it on their timetable and not before. They know WWIIers have "been there" and "done that," and they want to learn a lot from them; however it needs to be upon request. They cringe at the Boomers' slow and inefficient work habits and poor technical abilities and inform us that often these workaholic Baby Boomers are too focused on what is in it for them. They do enjoy a "glass is half full" attitude. When it comes to the GenXers, they stiffen up a little when this group tries to tell them how to do something.

Although this is an overview of the problematic attitudes each generation may have for another, the bottom line is that people are what make a company successful. The better people know how to work with each other, respect one another's differences of opinion and world viewpoints, the more they bring out the best in each other. Good people, who produce results and fit into the culture of a company, are critical to its success. These same good people know they are in high demand and they feel they have the freedom and talent to demand the right job on the right team, with the right company. They require a healthy, stimulating relationship with their manager or will leave when that is missing.

Regardless of the year someone was born, or the generation that formulated his or her attitudes, values and behavior; competitive and astute workers of every age have adopted a "free-agent" mentality and are building their relationships outside the company with vendors, customers, and ex-employees. People are connected to their community much easier today through LinkedIn and Facebook, so they are always ahead of the networking curve, and when the need arises, they typically land a new job fast. Companies that know this, and managers who create a community of diversity, reach more success in retaining these free agents than those companies that do not work on generational balance.

Working Together

You might not feel that age has a place in a discussion in business (there are rules and laws that forbid discrimination based on age), but for the first time in U.S. history, we have four generations, and soon to be five in the workforce. This discussion is not to promote stereotypes. The point is: age does not impact performance at all. Regardless of a person's age, if they have the competency to do the job, a robust capacity to learn, possess values that are congruent with the company's, and their behaviors and work style match the role, they have an excellent opportunity to shine in the position and with the company.

The challenge of building high performing teams occurs when management is unaware of how life and environmental dynamics affect the way different generations view the world, work with each other, and communicate. Inherently, these generations also have certain attitudes toward one another, that good coaching and awareness can help dissipate. In the Talent Management consulting field, most of the complaints we hear surround the communication and generational gaps that exist in the workforce.

21st Century Leadership & Employee Retention

Impacting your company's ability to retain key contributors, mission-critical players and next-level leaders begins with understanding your people from a demographic and psychographic point of view. In many ways, it's about the leaders in your organization demonstrating emotional intelligence and balanced decision making. When your leaders understand how their decisions affect the people, the tasks and the system overall, they make better decisions

Corporate Culture – Your Competitive Advantage

One of the most compelling and disturbing issues affecting the workplace today is the lack of employee engagement. The media call it the Blue Monday syndrome, psychologists call it employee resignation, and business leaders call it poor performance. Fractured employee engagement shows up in many different ways in the workplace. It can come in the form of extraneous people insights, the marketing department skipping out on optional fun team events, having no suggestions in the suggestion box, or it could show up in overall company trends. These problems result in complacency throughout the organization, just-under target performance, or an increase in missed deadlines, production or quality problems. The bottom line is that engagement is hijacked when an employee moves from productive to complacent.

People are complex; we are multifaceted, neurological and emotional beings. Therefore, it is essential to know what makes your people tick so that the redundancy of the corporate workspace and time does not overshadow who people are, why they said yes to the job, and what they need from their work. Good managers need to create a culture where people connect to the company mission, vision, and purpose, and convey the employee's unique contribution to the fulfillment of it to keep people productive, Absence of good people management and leadership causes the gestation and pervasiveness of these engagement hijackers.

In most situations, throughout all levels of engagement and

for most of your workforce, one thing is certain: the old form of corporate loyalty is dead. SHRM national survey results from 2012 and 2014, reported that the most significant trend most likely to have a strategic impact on how human resources functions is the growing need to develop retention strategies for mission-critical players, key contributors, and next-level leaders. What is essential to note is that **the problem is not going away.** As the economy gets better and hiring increases, the problem continues to grow.

In a disengaged workforce, on average, 75% of employees surveyed by CareerBuilder and high potentials and management personnel, say that if the phone rang tomorrow with a better opportunity, they would be more than open to taking the call and acting on it. In contrast, Gallup recently published that companies whose leaders emphasized culture increased in performance 202%. Also, the earning increase for companies with actively engaged employees showed an increase of 147%. What we can assert based on the numbers and trends is that if you want to stay competitive in business, your human system (the people that make the organization what it is) is your most valued asset.

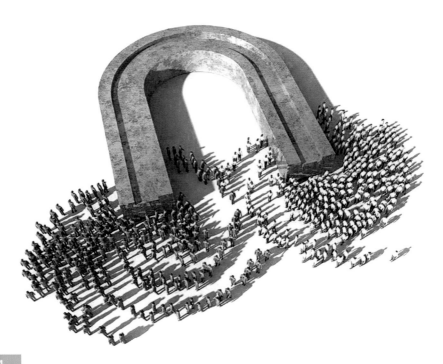

WORKFORCE OPTIMIZATION

Talent Strategy

Now is the time to choose if people are your competitive advantage, and if they are, you must strategically cause a corporate transformation, adopt a talent mindset and lead the way. Once you adopt and engage the rest of the leadership and management team in a talent mindset, the next step is to develop a talent strategy that lives and breathes throughout the organization.

A well-developed talent strategy includes:

1. Defined employment brand
2. Workforce planning
3. Ongoing recruitment initiatives
4. Systemic internal hiring process
5. Structure for accountability
6. Performance management system
7. Employee development program
8. Strong retention strategy

While small and mid-sized companies have been surviving, their larger and well-resourced competitors have been building and leveraging their people (talent) strategy and are thriving. The good news is that not every key contributor, mission-critical team member and next-level leader chooses to work for larger companies and mega-organizations. In all actuality, many have grown despondent and mistrustful of the larger entities and all too often, good workers with fast growth companies look to make a change when the company they helped to build gets too big. This opens the door for solid workers, skilled in growing organizations, to move to start-ups and privately held mid-sized companies—and for those companies to capitalize on their unique strengths and perspectives.

Most companies in business today, if they are successful, are hiring. Given the amount of effort and investment needed to create compelling employee retention programs, companies need to evaluate and improve their internal hiring practices so that they are investing in resources that yield a return. If your organization requires solid employee talent in order to compete and grow, adopting a talent mindset and executing a talent strategy is key to your sustainability and success. Institutionalizing key workforce processes and sharing your "people successes" within your management and leadership team, promises to elevate your ability to achieve the results you want. Many of the highly skilled people that make up the 21st-century workforce want to work for companies that make a difference and don't waste resources.

It does not take a large investment to evaluate roadblocks and red tape that could be in the way of shaving five hours off your employees' task lists every month.

Making a commitment to evaluate meaningful and lean initiatives that inspire, engage and connect employees to the bigger picture more often than not proves effective in stirring things up and raising the energy. Many progressive companies are implementing systems, processes and structures that improve their employees' experience of the company.

Some of the most popular talent strategy initiatives that companies are rolling out are:

> Standardized quality of hire systems and processes for all new hires

> Structured conscious leadership training and development of emotional intelligence, new manager training and high potential mentoring programs

> Better management throughout the employment life cycle, starting with clear results required in jobs, to compelling and inspiring career pathing

> Cross-functional accountability for staffing and retention

> Lean recruiting

> Talent mindset and accountability cultural shift

> Training and coaching in optimized workforces through a compelling EVP, effective brand messaging, lean recruiting strategies, and 21st-century business and employee management principles

> Knowledge transfer programs connecting generations for the purpose of sharing life, business, industry, company and people wisdom

> Transformational shift in HR from the center of compliance to the bridge between business strategy and people

> Deployment of the "Families of Retention" (How to Become an Employer of Choice, Joyce Gioia and Roger E. Herman, 2000)

> Accountability mindset that includes heightened performance management awareness, training, technology and know-how throughout the company

> Intercultural awareness, sensitivity and diversity training and coaching

Purpose & Meaning

Talent strategy begins with creating a vision for the difference your company wants to make, and asking employees for their ideas. As mentioned before; when you build your talent strategy, it is important to harness Stephen Covey's coaching (**stephencovey.com**) and begin with the end in mind. What is the result you want to accomplish and how will a robust talent strategy enable those accomplishments? Ask your key people what they want and which ideas inspire them. Conduct confidential employee check-in visits. Consider working with employees to develop professional growth goals and objectives around key initiatives; they will see themselves as part of the larger entity. When people are treated as key contributors and their opinions and ideas matter, performance and engagement ignite.

Everyone wants meaning and purpose in their lives. The 21st-century employee wants a company that leverages collaboration and teamwork. Open workspace promotes collaboration, creative problem solving and open lines of communication, as well as stronger opportunities for mentoring and on-the-job coaching. Given that the average person spends close to 80% of their waking hours at work, many people seek meaning and purpose at work; the companies that have figured this out have tapped into the core drivers of their key contributors and build the employee experience around those drivers. They have harnessed the real staying power of a solid retention strategy.

As Jim Collins writes, "It's about hiring great people and then getting out of their way. Create cross-functional teams to address issues with service delivery, production, product innovation, recruitment, etc. A great way to do this is to institute committees for creative problem-solving; a great venue to do this in is the virtual world, which creates a safe space for collaboration and creativity with little or no judgment" (Good to Great, 2001). To create a space for collaboration, consider removing the cubicles, as most people who choose to come to an office want to work with other people.

Another method of creating unification and buy-in is to use open-book management (**openbook-management.com**). Open-book management (OBM) is a management phrase coined by John Case of Inc. Magazine in 1993, then popularized by Jack Stack and his team at SRC Holdings. Many companies that practice open-book begin by teaching their employees basic financial literacy; they ensure their employees know the dynamics of supply and demand as well as profit and loss. When they open the books to a new person, they make sure the employee can read and understand profit and loss.

Keeping It Lean

Incorporating lean initiatives, or streamlining your operation, is to do more in less time with less effort. Talk to your people and look at what you can do to eliminate and simplify process and procedure. Determine where you can remove red tape and bureaucracy in the decision-making and customer service processes. If you can increase the amount of non-essential work processed for less expense, and there is no impact on your business model, your employees will appreciate your financial and operational discernment.

If outsourcing is just too risky for your company, insourcing is another cost-effective solution. Insourcing brings in consultants, contractors or third-party partners and allocates specific steps or all steps of a process to them. This tactic is often used heavily to augment existing staff or to manage a unique one-time project. The use of contractors frees your people to do what keeps them closest to strategy and do what they do best.

Practice Conscientiousness

Be environmentally conscious. Evaluate where you can "go paperless." The younger generation especially does not want to work for wasteful organizations that print and file hard copies. With the exponential growth of cloud storage like DropBox and Google, the need for paper files is waning. Your workforce wants to go green because they think printing is wasteful and filing is boring, while others see the world as being available at their fingertips no matter where their fingertips are, and for these employees having access to virtual cloud files works better.

It might make sense to reduce the carbon footprint, your employee's expense accounts and your employee's time away from loved ones. To do this, implement virtual meetings. With today's technology, you can hold meetings in a virtual world such as the wildly creative avenue of Second Life (**secondlife.com**) or the brass tacks of GoToMeeting (**gotomeeting.com**).

Lastly, many companies have past peak performers and key contributors who moved on and may now be retired. If those people were go-getters, they are probably are bored out of their minds and would enjoy the mental stimulation and challenge that a mentoring or part-time project opportunity could provide.

Employee Retention Strategies

Depending on your company, the culture and the individuals operating inside, you can employ one or all of the families of retention and experience exciting results.

Many of these families overlap with one another, as they are all about people, and ultimately most people are wired to want similar things. For each family of retention are many simple and complex programs you can roll out.

Environmental

➤ Clarify your company's mission, vision, and values. Share these in a simple and inspirational manner with your people in a public setting.

➤ Define your EVP; tie everything your company stands for and your company's purpose into it and exploit the reasons people say yes and the reasons they stay.

➤ Ensure proper employer branding; make sure the career page of your website maximizes your brand. If you say you treat people as individuals, but you have a generic and sterile application process, your words are incongruent with your method. Align them.

➤ Promote integrity and ethical business practices. Of course, if you hire highly ethical people, they demonstrate the opposite, unwanted turnover is the result.

➤ Conduct turnover statistics, including exit and stay interviews, and analyze the data. Share it, learn from it, make changes where needed, and exploit the good news.

➤ Maintain a safe, secure and comfortable work atmosphere and physical space. Installing ergonomic workstations is a great way to show you care.

➤ Life/work navigation needs to be a key element in your retention strategy. Concerned companies use common sense and demonstrate respect for their employee's multitude of commitments. People appreciate their manager for considering the impact of missing either their business or family priorities.

➤ Develop comprehensive talent acquisition and selection processes. Great people want to work with other great people. This statement is clear when it comes to sports teams and personal endeavors. It is the same in the workplace: build a team of winners with shared values and visions and watch everyone flourish.

➤ Operate with a talent mindset. Hire a management team who fundamentally believes that the company is only as good as the people inside. You cannot train someone who isn't philosophically aligned with this value to be a great manager and leader.

- Make your workplace engaging, fun and rewarding. Give people opportunities to stretch, get involved and be part of something bigger than themselves..

Relationship

- Know why people work for you.

- Organization. When you ask, you uncover elements of your employment brand that you can accentuate in your EVP.

- Understand the behavioral and thinking styles of your people and train your managers to do the same. As stated earlier: knowing what makes someone tick and how he or she best operates elevates your ability to communicate with your people and keep them engaged.

- Define the key roles in the organization, KPIs for the roles, and core accountabilities for those roles. Then define how you will know when you find the right person to fill one of those roles.

- Proactively resolve conflicts and turf battles at the moment they occur. Left unattended, this can cripple an organization and cause unwanted turnover.

- Regularly facilitate open communication between managers, business leaders, and team members. If your business is a bureaucracy, you will inadvertently attract and retain followers, not leaders.

- Build trust and partnership with your employees/ workforce.

- Show caring for people as individuals. Make sure your managers are empathetic enough to recognize and distinguish when an employee is in personal or professional trouble.

- Strengthen onboarding and employee bonding programs. Let the people you hire know the big "why" of your company mission: why they were hired, why people stay and why they ought to stay and career path with you.

- Invest in the "boomerang" principle: bring back people who once left the organization on good terms. Keep in mind that markets change, situations change, players change, and people change.

- Create opportunities for internal socialization: establish a Facebook or Meetup page for your employees to share, host employee collaboration state of the union meetings, and plan monthly employee socials. Create team fundraising events and work toward a cause.

Support

➤ Avoid "mushroom management." Mushrooms flourish in the dark; people don't. Don't keep people in the dark; let them know what is happening. If you don't tell them, they will make up a disempowering interpretation and waste time thinking about it.

➤ Reduce uncertainty and instability; tell people what is going on and where the company stands. Open the lines of communication about how the company addresses critical strategic issues and barriers to growth.

➤ Remove barriers to accomplishing tasks by conducting organizational assessments and 360s (in-depth interviews). Find out what processes are legacy based, outdated and need to go.

STRATEGY

INNOVATION

GROWTH

VISION

RESEARCH

TEAM WORK

➤ When you have a broad enough headcount, adjust specific jobs to fit strengths and talents. Consider the benefit of a having a utility player to support team efforts.

➤ Provide resources to get the work done, whether it's new tech, part-time support or streamlined systems. If you help people get more done in less time, everyone wins.

➤ Encourage and welcome new ideas. Each person has a different approach to getting work done. Listen to all methods and implement the best solution.

➤ Involve employees in decision making and problem-solving, as they are the people doing the work and they know best how to improve outcomes.

➤ Provide critical employees, who are personally accountable and responsible, with flexible scheduling, telecommuting or virtual work opportunities when appropriate.

➤ Build support strategies into your employment brand. Make sure your current and future employees know that you value them as individual contributors and that their opinions count. These people will be the ones sending you employee referrals, and those payoffs are huge.

Growth

➤ Identify your employees' career goals and objectives at the beginning of your relationship. This act ensures they know your company is aware of where they are going and encourages them to keep their eyes on the prize and stay connected with the company. When employees are present to their growth plan they operate more times than not with the end in mind and their engagement and performance improves exponentially.

➤ Create development plans for each key contributor within your organization. The creation of a plan brings life the responsibility for their growth and development. People who know where they are headed are more likely to get there.

➤ Establish a learning organization dedicated to continuous improvement. Provide training and cross-functional experiences. For example, "Walk a Mile in My Shoes" is a great program (**tangotraining.com**).

➤ Assist people in self-development. Self-esteem and emotional intelligence training, for example, is one of the best investments a company can make in their people. Healthy self-esteem and the ability to appropriately react to the pressures of life impacts performance, communication, teamwork, and goal accomplishment.

➤ Engage in succession planning: build the "bench" and develop your next-level leaders. If you value them, so will your competitors. People are less likely to look out the window or accept a cold call from a recruiter when they see the light at the end of the tunnel and are in a company-sponsored development, mentoring or coaching program.

➤ Develop structured on-the-job training programs. The biggest trigger of early defecting from a new job is when companies throw people in with little or no role training and no attention to employee integration.

➤ Develop coaching and mentoring programs. A great coaching and mentoring program matches the individual with the right coach or mentor, who can challenge the participant while stretching and guiding them to the next level. A great coaching program begins with a thorough assessment of the participant and the participant's manager (preferably a 360) and specific targeted outcomes.

Compensation

➤ Perform competitive compensation analysis and then make appropriate adjustments as needed.

➤ Communicate the full value of compensation, benefits, paid time off, training and 401k, and allocate a line item for everything you offer so your employees understand and see in writing what your company is investing in on their behalf.

➤ Establish a pay-for-performance program that expands all levels of the organization. When your company focuses on performance and rewards for performance, people respond.

➤ There is no one-shoe-fits-all regarding benefits anymore. Companies that use a flexible benefits plan and respond to a changing workforce have higher levels of participation and gratification.

➤ Explore options for nonfinancial compensation. Options may include paid time off, subsidized lunches, training and coaching programs, and/or participation in special "highly visible" projects that earn the employee status and recognition among their peers.

➤ Provide childcare and/or assistance with finding and paying for childcare costs.

➤ Offer other services to free up time and energy (laundry, car tune-ups, car wash, etc.).

➤ Beyond the five families and all that they entail, other initiatives that impact the quality and engagement of your workforce are systems that make work lean and programs that create work that is meaningful.

CONCLUSION

If you found this information valuable and would like to learn more, Keen Alignment offers on-site coaching and consulting to HR Services, Talent Acquisition departments and business leaders who want to shift from a tactical to a strategic mode of people operations. Additionally, Keen's Institute brings hundreds of human systems and leadership online courses that promise to raise your competence, expand your capacity and up-level your leadership.

FROM THE AUTHOR

In my 25 plus years as a Recruitment and Talent Management professional, I have an excellent track record of placing great people with innovative, successful companies. I operated for the first of those years primarily as a top-producing recruitment consultant and recruiting trainer. My career shifted towards the Quality of Hire track when I attended UIC's Masters in Business Administration program and I had to document my unique selling proposition and core business processes.

When I started the Conscious Hiring adventure, it was my mission to transform the recruiting and staffing industry, to raise our industry's level of influence, contribution and effectiveness. In a very short period of time, it was clear to me that the demand is not compelling at the staffing level; the demand is extraordinary at the corporate hiring level. Additionally, over the years of consulting and teaching people how to hire better, it has become ever so apparent that managers across the world are starving to get better. They are well aware that the impact of poor hiring, weak performance accountability and inadequate ability to inspire employees cripples their ability to accelerate their career. Our customers at KeenAlignment have helped us prove the claim that Conscious Hiring empowers employers to hire right, and employees to choose their next career opportunity wisely. It reduces new hire ramp-up time, improves employee engagement, raises employee productivity and strengthens engagement. When you choose the Conscious Hiring system, your company also reaps these benefits.

About Margaret Graziano

Margaret is a leading talent management expert, keynote speaker, and Chief Evangelist of KeenAlignment. KeenAlignment is an Inc. 5000 award recipient, being recognized as one of the fastest-growing private companies in America. A pioneer in her field, she has developed a talent strategy system that gives business leaders the actionable steps they need to align their corporate strategy with their people strategy and thereby maximize employee effectiveness and engagement and develop high performing teams who consistently elevate the customer experience.

ABOUT KEEN ALIGNMENT

At KeenAlignment, we integrate people and strategic resources to shape constructive high-performing cultures. Our plug-and-play Talent Management solutions align your people, optimize their contribution and accelerate your business plan. Through our customized educational programs and technology, we transform and elevate your human systems and make your company a best place to work.

Our Mission, Vision, Values & Operating Promise

WHO WE ARE

KeenAlignment is a collaborative group of highly successful Management Consulting Professionals with a collective commitment to transform and elevate all that is possible for a world at work.

OUR MISSION

We improve collaboration, empower momentum and elevate organizational performance through aligning people, purpose and strategy.

OUR VISION

Our vision is to create a new standard for empowered and optimized workplaces by introducing and implementing transformative Cultural Alignment programs, Human Systems Engineering, Conscious Hiring® methodology and 21st Century Leadership strategies.

OUR VALUES

➢ **Empowerment** - We take 100% responsibility for our impact and the difference we promise to make.

➢ **Excellence** - We are committed to delivering superior work product.

➢ **Service** - We equip and prepare our customers to unleash and optimize their leadership talent.

➢ **Transformation** - We evoke transformation in the people we work with.

➢ **Integrity** - We are honest, forthright, and do what we say we will do.

➢ **Results** - Our work optimizes people's contribution in the workplace and in their lives.

➢ **Humility** – We are humble, we own our successes as well as our failures; we clean up messes and choose to begin again.

OUR OPERATING PROMISE

We are a socially responsible company that enables HR and business values – driven leaders to come together and unleash the wealth of talent in the workplace, and mindfully build, shape, grow and scale for success.

To learn more, contact our team at (888)484-5551 or visit our website at: **www.keenalignment.com**

NOTES

Made in the USA
Lexington, KY
23 October 2019